What Others Are Saying

Close Kids is a very refreshing and insightful book to read. In today's world of limited family time, not only do parents not have the time to spend with their children, but siblings also do not have time to bond. As a pediatrician, I see this all too often. Bravo to Brett for researching this problem and bringing it to light.

I believe everyone who reads this book will be glad they did and will discover things they missed in their upbringing. *Close Kids* is an important resource for all parents!

—Richard Stanford, MD
Winner, Top 100 Pediatricians in America

A truly well written and organized book emphasizing the proper analogies for raising siblings to retain a close relationship. The book emphasizes important magnets that parents need to recognize in order to keep their children on the right track.

An excellent book every parent should read if they value family ties and relationships.

—James Cox, M.Ed.

I was surprised, satisfied, altogether pleased. I don't recall having encountered any earlier book or even a magazine article on the same theme…quite accomplished writing. I particularly liked all your carefully selected quotes from Rilke, Hepburn, Patton, Carlyle, and Hope. Full speed ahead…

—Larry Swindell
Ret. Book Critic, Fort Worth *Star Telegram,*
and bestselling author

The book is a brilliant, simple idea and a hot felt need. My wife and the kids' grandma are your sweet spots for sure.

—Bruce R. Barbour
Literary Agent, Literary Management Group

CLOSE KIDS

CLOSE KIDS

CONNECT YOUR CHILDREN FOR LIFE

BRETT A. JOHNSTON

Tate Publishing & *Enterprises*

Published by Tate Publishing & Enterprises, LLC
127 E. Trade Center Terrace | Mustang, Oklahoma 73064 USA
1.888.361.9473 | www.tatepublishing.com

Tate Publishing is committed to excellence in the publishing industry. The company reflects the philosophy established by the founders, based on Psalm 68:11,
"The Lord gave the word and great was the company of those who published it."

Cover design by Lance Waldrop
Interior design by Jeff Fisher
Cover Photograph by Cindy Ritchie

Published in the United States of America

ISBN: 978-1-61566-080-3
1. Family & Relationships, Siblings
2. Family & Relationships, Family relationships
09.10.06

Dedication

This book is dedicated to all the
wonderful, strong, and interesting women
in my life whom I love dearly:

Tiffini

Sondra, Nancy

Drew, Tatum, and Evan.

ACKNOWLEDGEMENTS

Dear friends, I would be remiss if I didn't take a moment to thank all the people who made this project what it is. No single act by me was responsible, and in many ways, this work came from somewhere outside my consciousness. There are many people to thank for their time, energy, and creativity who made this book happen.

Tiffini Johnston

Mony Cunningham

Glynne Johnston

Sondra Johnston

Nancy Stanford

Angie Miller

Vicky Gourgouri

Dr. Gordon McClellan

Krista McClellan

James & Sue Cox

Dr. Richard Stanford

Pat Deason

Helen Holmes

James Bost

David Wood

Larry Swindell

Bruce Barbour

Jaime McNutt Bode

Lance Waldrop

Jeff Fisher

Cindy Ritchie

And everyone I know and didn't know who I asked, "Are you close to your siblings?"

And most of all God for putting so many obstacles in my path, which changed the direction I was going so many times. Thank you.

TABLE OF CONTENTS

Introduction

> Be patient toward all that is unsolved in your heart and try to love the questions themselves ... And the point is to live everything. Live the questions.
>
> —Rainer Maria Rilke,
> *Letters to a Young Poet*

Becoming a father brought not only a precious little bundle of joy into my life but a bundle of questions and challenges about parenting that tiny human being, about how to provide the best nurturing and environment possible. As other little bundles joined our family, along came more questions and challenges. It has been a great and satisfying adventure to face and accept some of those challenges, ask the questions, and discover some of the answers—an adventure that I realize will continue throughout my lifetime.

This book is the result of this father's quest to answer one of those questions, to "live the question."

> What can my wife and I do with our young children today to provide them the best chance of having a solid, loving, and close relationship with each other as adults?

The following pages hold the nuggets I have discovered so far on my journey. Let me begin by telling you how this particular project came to be. My wife, Tiffini, and I were discussing a friend of ours and her extraordinarily close relationship to her sister. These two thirty-something sisters are inseparable. Their bond is so great neither one makes a big decision without bouncing the idea off their "best friend." The sisters check on each other often to talk about the small events of life or just to say hello.

Each has her own family with children and is perfectly attentive and capable of handling her own affairs, but there is something special about the way they communicate and lean on each other. We thought how nice it would be for our girls to grow up and enjoy this type of relationship!

Tiffini and I started asking the sisters questions about their great connection. We asked about how they were raised. Did they just happen to like the same things or have similar views that gave them common areas of interest? Did specific events take place during their childhood to strengthen their relationship? What, if anything, did their parents do to support and foster their budding friendship?

These sisters had a lot of the same things in common as other people we knew. As we thought about it, we could name other friends with similarly great adult relationships. Some were sisters, some were brothers, and some were a mix. We could also name a few friends that had downright poor relationships. Why was there such a disparity between similar adults in a relationship that *should* be the closest one we have outside of our relationship with our spouse?

Never fear, I thought. In this day and age, the answers to any question are just a few clicks away, right? I would easily find the information needed to ensure our girls a lifetime of friendship right on the Internet. Wrong. Not this time. After checking the usual places for books about "close kids" or "close siblings," nothing came up—not a single book or even an article.

Now, there are literally thousands of books on parenting and raising children, and I've enjoyed reading many of them. They address everything from overcoming a temper tantrum to "Training a Tiger." There are so many I sometimes have trouble making a selection. One similarity reigns supreme through almost all of them. *They are oriented in the present.* This is fine but not what I was looking for. I wanted to delve into the future, to learn something today that would help my kids form a lifelong bond with each other. Was it possible?

With little to no input available from existing materials, I realized I would have to come up with a plan to find the information. My solution was to develop a massive, Internet-based survey. As ideas formulated for collecting data, a realization came to me. *In almost every single case, in every country around the world, the sibling relationship is the longest relationship of anyone's life.* Chances are most siblings will not know their spouses for nearly as long as they will know each other—all the more reason it should be a joyful and rich experience!

The original idea was pretty simple: find a way to gather a large amount of information on siblings; separate the responses into two groups, placing those with great relationships in one pile and those with poor relationships in pile number two; then look into the time respondents spent together under one roof with their siblings, specifically their time spent at home from age zero to eighteen; and see what information could be uncovered.

My hope was that the key findings from the "close sibling group" could be pulled out and applied to my family today, that they would prove to be transferable and reproducible. Those key principles could then be used as a guide to give our kids the best shot at a close, lifelong relationship.

The electronic survey was finished and traveled around the world in no time flat! The response to the survey and subject matter was overwhelming. People from all over the world participated—from mainland USA to New Zealand, Australia, the Orient, then on to Europe and Africa. The flood of information was off the charts! Individuals were sharing the survey with friends and family, asking questions and dying to hear the results. This response was both gratifying and humbling.

We want our kids to have a bond that will stand the test of time, life's unexpected tragedies, bad hair days (we have three girls), boyfriends (I'm willing to wait a *long* time for those problems), their own kids, or anything else life brings their way. By positively impacting the way our children relate to each other, we can also positively impact their interaction with us and others, which may bring even more value to the small lessons of this book.

Because this subject is my passion and many others seemed to be interested, it became my goal to make the key findings available to the world in the book you now hold. I hope you will use it as a reference for years to come and deem it worthy of sharing with your friends.

WHAT THIS BOOK IS

The goal of this book is to provide you with tools and ideas to help give your children the awesome gift of a positive, lifelong relationship together. Parents have a huge impact on the ultimate relationship of their children, and I firmly believe the more "CloseKids" principles utilized in a family, the better chance siblings will have to become close kids for life.

WHAT THIS BOOK IS NOT

If your children are in need of professional help, this book is not your answer. CloseKids.com is currently teaming up with professional family therapists around the country to create a network of people who can help you. As a service to our customers, we are compiling a list of certified professional family counselors throughout the country. Visit our Web site to see if there is one in your neighborhood. We will do everything in our power to help you and your children.

SOMETHING BIGGER THAN THIS BOOK

Part of the proceeds of this book will go to help organizations that make a real difference in the lives of kids. It became evident during this process that I needed to step up and teach my kids about giving to others. Groups that reach out to help kids learn about giving are very near to my heart, and I want to share them with my children and your family. So if you know of a group that you think helps kids in a special way, please let me know at CloseKids.com. I would love to hear from you and consider them as a future partner!

Why We Lose Connection

One goal of this project is to bring hope to those of you who do not have close connections with your siblings. The ideas in this book are not only to inspire you to help your children build better relationships but to give you some understanding of how you can turn your own sibling relationships into closer connections. Toward that end, I want to mention a few items specifically noted as being major contributors to poor relationships among siblings as adults. Hopefully, by looking at these, you can better examine your current situation and make adjustments as necessary.

The number one reason adults cited for a poor connection with their siblings was the *lack of time* available. We run kids here, there, and there again; work extra jobs to earn more money; run home businesses; study finances; and fold clothes (and fold more clothes). Since you have kids, you know exactly what I'm talking about. So as adults trying to keep in contact with our siblings, time is a real factor. As you can imagine, free time to interact plays a part in the sibling relationship from an early age. Later in this book, you will learn and be well armed with ideas and solutions to overcome this pesky issue. Kids will learn spending time together is "just something we do."

Another factor working against us is *technology.* Some obvious examples are TVs and computers. Computers can isolate the user from other people because they are not typically used by more than one person at a time. My kids do not need and often do not want interaction with their sisters when they surf the Internet, play a game on the computer, or watch TV. Certainly, this differs from past childhood norms where real entertainment—sometimes the only entertainment—was found in each other. Obviously, we cannot go backward in time, but keeping a watchful eye on computer time or games that isolate children is prudent.

As other technology moves forward, even family vacations may not include as much time together as they used to. For example, with the advent of personal DVD players and iPods, it is possible for a family to be in a car for hours and never say a word to each other. Each person in the family *could* have their own headphones on and watch or listen to their own movie or music. What used to be four hours in the car of talking to each other could become four hours of potential seclusion. Are we creating an environment of togetherness with technology? I'm not sure but, logically thinking, probably not.

I spoke to a physician friend of mine about this particular subject recently. After laughing about spending time not spending time together, he made a real-world point. He said, "The world is so much more difficult to manage today. Most people are so worn out by the end of the day they are looking for any refuge of peace. Unfortunately, many people find peace in solidarity. You *should* probably look for peace within your family."

As with most lessons, parents actually have to teach their children how to spend time together. It may take some effort and planning, but putting children in situations where they just play and enjoy each other's company is a great thing. While this is certainly not a novel idea, it is, in practice, often overlooked.

There is no evil in a child listening to music or watching a movie. There is a lesson in learning the ability to be happy doing your own thing. The challenge is for parents to find balance in what we let children do. Balance time together, balance time alone, and balance the million and one other things going on in a family. Balance is ultimately found by recognizing all the different activities your crew is doing and not being dominated by a few.

Physical distance apart was another factor survey respondents thought kept them from being emotionally tied to their siblings.

While I found this to be a fairly common statement when I talk to parents, distance apart was not a statistically significant factor in my study. Being close or not close emotionally really transcends geographical distance—distance is what you make of it and not a real reason to lose touch with a brother or sister. Certainly, it is harder to get together in person when everyone is spread out to the four corners, but there are many ways to cope with distance in a positive way. In fact, this is an instance when technology can play a positive role in staying connected.

A good friend of mine and his rather large group of siblings live as spread out as could possibly be. They have a great tradition that keeps them together and interacting year after year. Each year, a different sibling chooses a place for the family to vacation together. Everyone tries very hard to make the trip every year and bring his or her entire family. Once they arrive, one couple is responsible for all three meals on *one* given day. This takes most of the stress out of planning meals, and they just get to hang out, relax, and enjoy each other. This story is a real-world example showing that distance does not have to get in the way of family. They are actively overcoming their physical locations and sticking together.

With the advent of Internet connection sites, physical distance is becoming even more irrelevant. Can't make the trip this year? Use Face-

Book to upload some pictures to your family. Have separated parents who don't get together? Share a MySpace page or send them a Tweet. The options are truly endless!

Religion is another factor influencing adult sibling relationships. Siblings sometimes take different paths, and their religious beliefs or a lack thereof can certainly cause conflict and separation. It should be said that it can also bring brothers and sisters together. As I point out later in the book, religion is a very strong contributor to having a close set of children. But it must be noted that religion used in the wrong way can have a detrimental effect on these relationships.

Finally, *longstanding family problems* were another major cause of riffs. Many specific examples were given, but the top response was clearly money. As we all know, money can make normal people act anything but normal! Many siblings "keep score," fighting over a few bucks here and there, not realizing what it does to their relationship. After reading their specific reasoning, the root cause of the poor relationship seemed to be more about selfishness than money. And we devote an entire chapter to this later in the book so selfish behavior is kept at a minimum in your family!

I thought it was important to share some of these negative relationship influences up front for a few reasons. First, it is interesting to see what separates some siblings and what others do to overcome those obstacles. Second, they help raise parents' awareness about hidden events that could impact their children's relationships. Finally, there is so much fun stuff coming I want everything from here on out positive, upbeat, and captivating enough to keep you turning the pages all the way to the end!

Beyond Our Control

Because we as mortals cannot control certain things about our kids—gender, physical attributes, birth date, etc.—the following might be nothing more than simply interesting. However, the survey allowed some conclusions to a few age-old questions.

IS THE MORE REALLY THE MERRIER?

We have always heard, "The more the merrier!" Is that really true? (Are they talking about kids or money?) Has anyone actually gathered data to prove if that old saying was right or wrong? Also, are girls really closer than boys? I've always heard they were.

Is the suspense getting to you yet? Well, here is the answer according to the information gathered. There is, in fact, a perfect trend showing as a new sibling is added to the family, the siblings *are* closer as adults. When you go from two to three, their "close rating" goes up. Those in our test group with four siblings? Up again. Five or more? Up yet again.

Whew! I have three, and we hardly get any rest! Maybe we need to start having kids to take care of the kids. I'll bring that one up with my wife. On second thought, being married for almost fifteen years has taught me there are some times it's best to keep quiet.

No one should make a decision on how many children they will have based on this score. It is interesting to know, however, that parents are not causing long-term or emotional pain to their kids when a new baby comes home from the hospital. The reverse, in fact, is strongly suggested by these figures.

ARE GIRLS REALLY CLOSER?

As a father of girls, I was interested in pulling out data that compared the sexes. Were girls really closer? Fortunately, it looks like nature has taken care of part of my concerns without me. I'm quite comfortable in saying the more girls in a group of siblings, the higher their close rating becomes. The data suggests an absolute perfect trend from one girl on up.

The close rating does not break if boys are in the mix. But looking at the facts, adding girls undoubtedly increases the rating of the siblings. This does not say that boys are not or cannot be close. There are all-boy families with close ratings of 10, and lots of them! So do not fear if you have sons. They can all be close! Why this difference exists is beyond the scope of the study.

IS AGE DIFFERENCE A FACTOR?

Another interesting fact for this section gives us the answers to these questions: "How close in age were the closest siblings? Would children born close to each other fare better than children born years and years apart?" The answer is that age distance does seem to matter. The closer the siblings were in age, the closer they were as adults. While probably not a surprise to most people, it is nice to see some proof for an age-old question.

We had, purely by accident, three children in three and a half years. *That is really close!* Changing diapers and cleaning up for three nearly killed us. Everyone always tells us, "Oh, they will be so close." But until this study was complete, it was really only nice conversation. Now it seems like the odds are lining up in their favor. According to the study, a one-and-a-half to two-and-a-half-year range between children is optimal.

DOES TRAUMA PLAY A ROLE?

I want to tell you about an unexpected story that really caught my attention from the open-ended section of the survey. While most of the questions were multiple choice, some people really elaborated on their personal experiences in this section. This part revealed what happens to children who experience family trauma like divorce, drug abuse, or the death of a parent or sibling. It was here that I received one of the most interesting and heart-wrenching stories.

The answer to my question was twofold. For the most part, traumatic events either drove kids together, making them ultra close, or they severely divided them. How can parents best deal with these problems? First, just knowing that traumatic family issues have a real impact on kids is a big step. Second, do not be afraid to seek professional help to make sure the children continue to feel loved, supported, and part of the family.

Okay. Now the story that I received from a woman named Grace who lives in Cincinnati.

She wrote:

> Brett, a friend of mine sent me a link to your sibling survey today. Since I grew up in a fam-

ily of five brothers and sisters, the topic was very interesting to me. After taking the multiple choice questions, I began to weep when I answered your question, "In your own words, why do you think you are close/not close to your siblings today?"

I realized why we are tied so closely together and have been our whole lives. Although it has been over fifty years since we lived in the same house together, I remember certain events of my childhood as if it was yesterday. My mother was very critical of us children and my father. He was actually very distant and probably would be considered an alcoholic. They had terrible fights that would last for days. Much of this time we spent huddled in a room together, too afraid to go out. If we came out too early, we received a harsh spanking or worse.

There were always threats of suicide and divorce. As crazy as it sounds, we were driven to lean entirely on each other. Our shared experience actually made us an incredibly tight group, even to this day. I hope this helps. Good luck.

—Grace–Cincinnati, OH

This moving story is proof of the power of siblings. I added it for two very specific reasons. First, it shows the resiliency of kids. These brothers and sisters were in a horrible situation. They not only survived, but they survived together and grew up with a great relationship. Second, it gives hope to the parents who think they might have done irrevocable harm to their children before reading this book. Have faith! Kids want to forgive you and build new connections with you and their siblings. There is always time to turn it around.

We Make Our Own Reality

> Never let someone's opinion of you become your reality.
>
> —Les Brown

Again, this chapter should serve as interesting background material, not necessarily something on which to base family decisions. Do not get discouraged if your children are not really close in age or you don't have many girls in your clan or for *any* other reason. These are only statistical similarities and *will not* determine your children's eventual relationship! Only you and they can do that.

The 8 CloseKids Factors

Action Items to Bond Your Children for Life!

Okay. Enough of the preliminaries. You're ready for the really juicy stuff, right? Over the next few pages are the *specific* practices of those families who produced the closest adult siblings. This information came directly from the survey. These practices are well defined, easy to do, repeatable, and even fun.

They are listed in order, starting with the most statistically significant. Included are the top eight factors revealed by the data. Do not, however, be overly concerned with how important one is over the other. Take the ones that seem the most applicable to you and implement them as you see fit.

CloseKids Factor 1:

Siblings' Support of Extracurricular Activities

In this hustle and bustle world, our children are involved in more activities than ever. The following practice never crossed my mind before this process started. That is the importance of making time for our children to support *each other* in their individual activities. This kind of information is exactly what I hoped to find when the journey began. This stuff makes me excited!

Giving kids the time to cheer for each other ended up being the strongest individual factor contributing to a close adult relationship. In fact, it is notably more essential for brothers and sisters to cheer on and support each other than it is for their parents to do the same thing. Parents supporting their kids' activities, while still a positive indicator for close adult siblings, only ranked somewhere in the middle of the pack in this study.

This is certainly not to say that parents do not have to support the activities of their children. The significance of them doing so is still high, and saying otherwise is wrong and not supported by my findings. The point is the whole family rooting for each other seems to promote an "us" mentality with the children versus an "I" mentality. The more "us" the better!

This idea may force parents to make some tough decisions. Juggling time between our kids can be like running a three-ring circus that would make even the Ringling Brothers proud. How much extracurricular activity is enough? Can we do all the things we want to do and still leave enough time to cheer and support each other as a family? These are complex questions each family must answer for itself. And I encourage you to make your choices as a family whenever possible. Although it might be logistically impossible for everyone to cheer for *every* activity in person, we can still support in spirit. Just remember to try to allow some time to root for the home team: each other!

On a personal note, we started clapping and cheering for the kids when they did something well (like singing a song or walking for the first time) and asking the others to chime in. It has been nice to watch the older ones carry the idea along on their own. They routinely clap for each other after "performances" and other activities. Our task is to continue the process and hope it sticks.

It also appears that *support* can mean several different things. Showing an interest in each other's activities during quiet times can be just as important as cheering during an actual event. So support does not only mean physical attendance but taking an interest outside the event as well. An example would be asking about a book someone is reading, taking an interest in a project together, or finding a gift that contributes to their special interest. There are many ways to make someone feel important by showing them support.

The easiest way to get this rolling in your family is to simply start the dialogue in any situation that might deserve it. You will be surprised at how quickly the kids follow your lead and start to enjoy cheering and supporting each other. It is great to see a child's eyes light up with joy when their siblings are excited about their accomplishments.

CLOSEKIDS FACTOR 2:

ALL SIBLINGS THOUGHT THEY HAD AN EQUAL VOICE

Next up on the agenda was giving each child the sense that his or her voice was heard. The survey respondents with the closest sibling relationships thought they had ample opportunity to speak their minds within their family, be heard, and have their opinions acted upon reasonably. There were many respondents who rated extremely low on the closeness scale (3 or less) who flat out said they were ignored when it came to making family decisions. Regardless of their age or input, what they said never carried any weight or received any real consideration.

As chance would have it, I was told a great story during the preparation of this book. I heard how the late John D. Rockefeller Sr. would make sure all of his children were given a chance to speak and hold the stage. He gave his children book reports or research projects to work on independently. When they finished, each child was expected to give a full presentation to the family at the dinner table on the night it was due. It might sound a bit over the top (I swing back and forth on it myself), but Mr. Rockefeller's idea certainly gave attention and the spotlight to each of his kids and forced the others to listen. Each child had a time to shine and have their voice heard.

Okay, it is understandable that most people may not take it that far. But are there other ways to achieve the same results in an easier way? Take a moment yourself and think of a few ideas that might work for your family, or, better yet, ask your family what they would suggest.

Although I certainly do not have all of the answers, here are a few we've tried in our home.

- Each child chooses a nighttime book for the family to read together.
- Everyone gets a chance to say his or her own prayer. (This has been a very satisfying, often humorous, and sometimes lengthy process. However, it gives you great insight into what kids really care about and are thankful and hopeful for.)

- We sing a bunch at our house, so each girl gets the chance to sing her song without interruption or input.
- Let the kids decide between several choices of a restaurant.
- Give kids the choice of what park they would like to visit.

There is so much more. Come share your ideas with us at CloseKids.com.

These are just a few things we are trying, but they seem to be working well. Our second child had a tough time at first with her verbal skills. It caused her to sit quietly and watch her older sister talk all day. When we started taking the time and putting forth the effort to give her center stage to speak, she really came into her own. I'm not sure who talks more between one and two, but I do know this. Number three has no problem making her voice heard, and she is only one!

CLOSEKIDS FACTOR 3:

THE FAMILY THAT PRAYS TOGETHER…

I'm sure most everyone reading this has heard the statement, "The family that prays together stays together." What I never could determine, until this survey, was how much truth there was in that statement. The declaration was made famous in the 1940s by Father Patrick Peyton on his World War II radio show. But famous words are not necessarily true.

The answer in terms of this book is a resounding yes. Praying together as a family ranked solidly in the number three position. Those respondents who said their families prayed together either "always" or "most of the time" had a much better chance of having a good relationship with their siblings as adults.

I'm not sure how much more information can be offered about this particular item. Either it is something you and your family are apt to do, or you're not. For those who obtain peace and happiness praying together, this finding represents an enormous reason to continue the tradition. For those on the fence, it might be the opportunity to make praying together a new habit.

There was a very significant side note I discovered late in the process of writing this book. I realized the divorce rates of my survey participants' parents could be compared to how much or how little their family prayed together. This would either prove or disprove the age-old saying, "The family that prays together stays together."

The divorce rate of families who prayed together either "all the time" or "most of the time" in my study was three times lower than those who prayed together either "seldom" or "never." In my opinion, this data strongly suggests the age-old statement is probably right on the mark.

CloseKids Factor 4:

Attending Religious Services Together

It seems a natural follow-up that attending religious services regularly as a family is next in line. Just a shade below praying together was attending religious services together. Again, I don't have much to add either way on this particular subject. However, these two factors should give added support to those families who want to attend services together more frequently and might need some added justification. Regardless of your religious preference, attending religious services of any kind, as a family, is a significant factor in how our children relate to each other as adults.

As this book was almost ready to go to press, I found a study of over sixteen thousand mostly first-graders that supported my findings. The research was headed by John Bartkowski of Mississippi State University. Mr. Bartkowski found, "Kids whose parents regularly attended religious services—especially when both parents did so frequently—and talked with their kids about religion were rated by both parents and teachers as having better self-control, social skills, and approaches to learning than kids with nonreligious parents."

CLOSEKIDS FACTOR 5:

READ ALOUD AS A FAMILY

Here is another factor that really surprised me. Reading aloud as a family had a very strong impact on connecting siblings. In fact, there is one way to crunch our data that makes this the number one trait on the list. Using an average of several calculation methods (which I did), it winds up at number five.

Our family tries very hard to read something together every night, but it can be hard getting kids to bed on time—even without reading! Our nightly ritual sounds a bit like this.

"Girls, let's brush our teeth so we can read a book, okay?"

"Drew, can you come to the bathroom so I can brush your teeth?"

"Drew?" (She was just here!)

"Tatum, can I brush your teeth ... please?"

"Tatum?"

"Tatum?"

"Hey, where did everyone go?"

"Evan?"

"I need to brush ... Huh? You are *still* looking for your blankie, Tatum?"

Under my breath, "I'm going to kill the person who invented blankies!"

"Let me brush Evan's teeth, and I'll help you look for it."

"Evan? Evan!"

The tasks at hand may involve finishing up homework or other projects due the next day, but basically it probably doesn't sound all that much different at your house. I totally understand. It is not easy getting all the nighttime activities completed at a reasonable hour. But if you look at the benefits of taking a little time to sit quietly together and listen to a good story, it is certainly worth the effort.

Usually the girls pick a book to read, but sometimes we have a favorite too. As they have grown older, it is natural they start doing the reading for the group. In fact, the youngest will not be outdone and has "read" all sorts of books during her time. Keep in mind, she can't read a lick yet, but she will tell a great story while she turns the pages. She is currently on a *Marley and Me* kick. She knows there is a dog in it, so every sentence uses the word *dog*.

Reading aloud also gives parents the awesome opportunity to bring together many aspects of this book. It fully allows the *opportunity* for kids to *have their voice heard* and might even create some *laughter!*

CLOSEKIDS FACTOR 6:

PLAYING WITH SIBLINGS OVER FRIENDS

Coming in at number six was the factor that individuals who scored highest on the study said they chose to play with their siblings more often than with neighborhood friends. Without further investigation, it is difficult to determine exactly why people chose to play with their brothers and sisters most often. Were there no other kids around? Did they have a large family? Were they geographically isolated so they *had* to play together? I don't know, and it really does not make much difference. What can be determined is the children definitely had the *opportunity* and *time* to interact in a playful environment as siblings.

It might be as simple as spending time together. As adults, we become closer to those people we spend our time with. I know I am naturally drawn to those I enjoy playing golf with. I find myself looking forward to spending a few hours with those individuals, even when it doesn't involve a game of golf.

You would think that giving our kids time to play together each day would not be hard to do. But, as we talked about earlier, finding some extra time in a day is not always easy. At our house, we are trying to ensure some downtime each day where our children have nothing else to do but interact with each other. Maybe we should declare it recess! Hey, recess for them, siesta for me? That might be a winner.

Here is a great way one of the survey respondents created time to put her brother not only over her friends but ultimately over herself.

> Brett, your survey reminded me of something my sister did that sealed our relationship for the better. My sister was quite a bit older than I was and in high school at the same time I was in grade school.
>
> There was a time when she seemed to go out every weekend and I never got to see her. I think she probably felt she was abandoning me so she made me an incredible offer. One I thought was wonderful then and view as nearly inconceivable now that I am older and understand the sacrifice she made as a mere teenager.

My sister, Katherine, told me one day she would never go out on Saturday nights without me. Friday night she would spend with her friends, but Saturday night was all mine. She never wavered and it was not an empty promise.

She and I would go exploring in Harriman State Park, take trips to Coney Island and I even remember her setting up the telescope in the front yard and teaching me about astronomy. She would make up songs and we had all sorts of inside jokes that we never included our parents in on. Even to this day, we still talk about all the things we did together.

We became extraordinarily close friends despite our age difference. It would have been easy for her to disappear from my life forever like some kids do. But she didn't. I tell my children often about all the great things my sister did with me. I hope and pray my daughter Samantha grows up with Aunt Katherine's wonderful heart.

—Ron
Yonkers, N.Y.

CLOSEKIDS FACTOR 7:

DINNERTIME

We have all heard about how important it is to eat together as a family. There are even studies dedicated to just how we communicate and bond around mealtime. What I had not seen before and surprised me is what goes on around the table *after* we eat. Scoring higher than just eating together and falling at number seven on the list was eating together *plus* continuing to sit and visit after the meal was done. Our study found families that spent an extra fifteen minutes together after dinner was done produced closer children than those who did not.

This brings images to my mind of movies about Italian families in Tuscany. They sit around a dinner table for hours sipping nice red wines from Piedmont and telling stories about life and love. There are many traditions that come to us from across the pond. Letting the dinner table be a catalyst for communication and bonding as a family is one custom you should definitely adopt at your house.

My wife's family is of German decent. I can say with certainty they do not have a problem staying at the table for hours after dinner! Both my buns and brains had to get used to all that sitting ... and talking. Four hours is certainly not a required act. All that is needed is some meaningful conversation when dinner is over. Sounds simple, right?

Again, this idea can be threatened by our demanding schedules. But even in the most hectic lives, there is always a way to add five or ten minutes' worth of this or that. It can be done. In some families, a good start would just be asking everyone to sit through an entire meal together and then gradually tacking on some conversation at the end. We are starting slowly, adding a few minutes after every meal. I do not know what will happen, but we are giving it a chance.

CLOSEKIDS FACTOR 8:

HAVING PARENTS WHO ARE CLOSE TO THEIR SIBLINGS

The final controllable factor that we are going to discuss is whether or not the parents being close to their siblings had any effect on their kids. The answer is yes. It can absolutely make a difference. It is probably common sense but not commonly thought about. Simply put, if we are close to our siblings, it is more likely our children will be close to each other. Our children learn more from our example than our words.

So, if you have a great sibling relationship, feel free to flaunt it to your kids. They will see the love you have for each other; learn how good brothers and sisters treat each other; and, in time, create close relationships themselves.

If you have less than desirable relationships with some members of your family, shielding the kids from those situations where you become frustrated or angry with a family member is perhaps a good idea. At least be careful while you are trying to mend any lingering issues. Finally, if you have an outright hostile relationship with your siblings, why bring your children into that situation at all? Isn't it our job to protect them at any cost?

Bringing your children into a situation you know is going to be bad may be placing them at risk. Rethink the decision. Ask yourself the following question. Is there enough of a positive impact in a given situation to outweigh the negative atmosphere they may be forced to deal with? If we *knew* our girls would be worse off by attending a family event, we would politely decline to attend. What would we have to lose anyway? Probably not much.

Finally, for those of you who were interested, statistically speaking, the data suggests that it is more significant for the father to be close to his siblings than the mother. While both are important and meaningful, fathers need to make sure they reach out to their family as well.

Wrapping It Up

Well, that represents the top eight factors that individuals just like you came up with that separated close siblings from those who were not. My hope is you found them interesting, helpful, and fun and you are excited to try some with your family! In a world that is pulling each of us in so many directions, I think you will find these help pull your family back together. Please drop me a line and let me know how they work for you.

I also want to share a final note about the research conclusions on having close kids. If you are at all like me, you are a bit skeptical about information you see these days. That is fine, and here is the bottom line on the Close Kids principles.

If you look at the seventy-five families from the study who enacted the eight ideas from this book the most, those children grew up to rate their sibling relationship an average of 8.8 out of 10. If you look at the bottom seventy-five families who completed these ideas the least, their children rated their adult sibling relationship only an average of 5.7 out of 10. The Close Kids principles work!

These factors are the results and side effects of an underlying truth that a family with a deliberate, strong, and consistent belief in what they are doing is the best environment for siblings to grow and prosper together. Parents who are confident and comfortable in their beliefs and model that behavior to their children will pass on to a generation of offspring a foundation for love, humility, and understanding.

Over twenty unique ideas came from the survey. If you are interested in viewing the others, please contact me at CloseKids.com. I will send you the additional information at no charge, and you can sign up for the free Close Kids Newsletter while you are there!

The Most Powerful Factor

Giving the Gift of a Great Childhood

Once the survey was finished and all the data had been sifted through, one factor stood out above all others in deciding whether or not children would grow up close. Implementing this one principle improved the "close rating" of an individual by around 33 percent. That is a 33 percent better chance of a positive sibling relationship as adults by just completing one thing!

The factor was *overall childhood experience.*

So my goal was to understand what parents, myself included, could do to help our kids score their childhood a 10 out of 10! But I had a problem. How could one accurately define a *good* overall childhood experience?

As I searched for some undeniable truths about creating a great foundation and environment for kids, a game plan came to mind. I returned to the surveys and took another look at those respondents who scored their childhood a perfect 10. What could I learn from them?

I was surprised to find the list you see below practically write itself. Words like *listening*, *acceptance*, and *forgiveness* seemed to leap off the pages. It wasn't long before a solid list came together.

See if you agree that any child (or adult for that matter) would thrive while living in these conditions. Parents who provide this kind of atmosphere are raising their child's potential to have a very good overall childhood experience. While some of these pillars do not overtly tie to sibling relationships, they create an underlying environment of super-connectivity in the house. A channel if you will where brothers and sisters have their basic needs taken care of and can spend their brain power on forming collective memories to cherish forever.

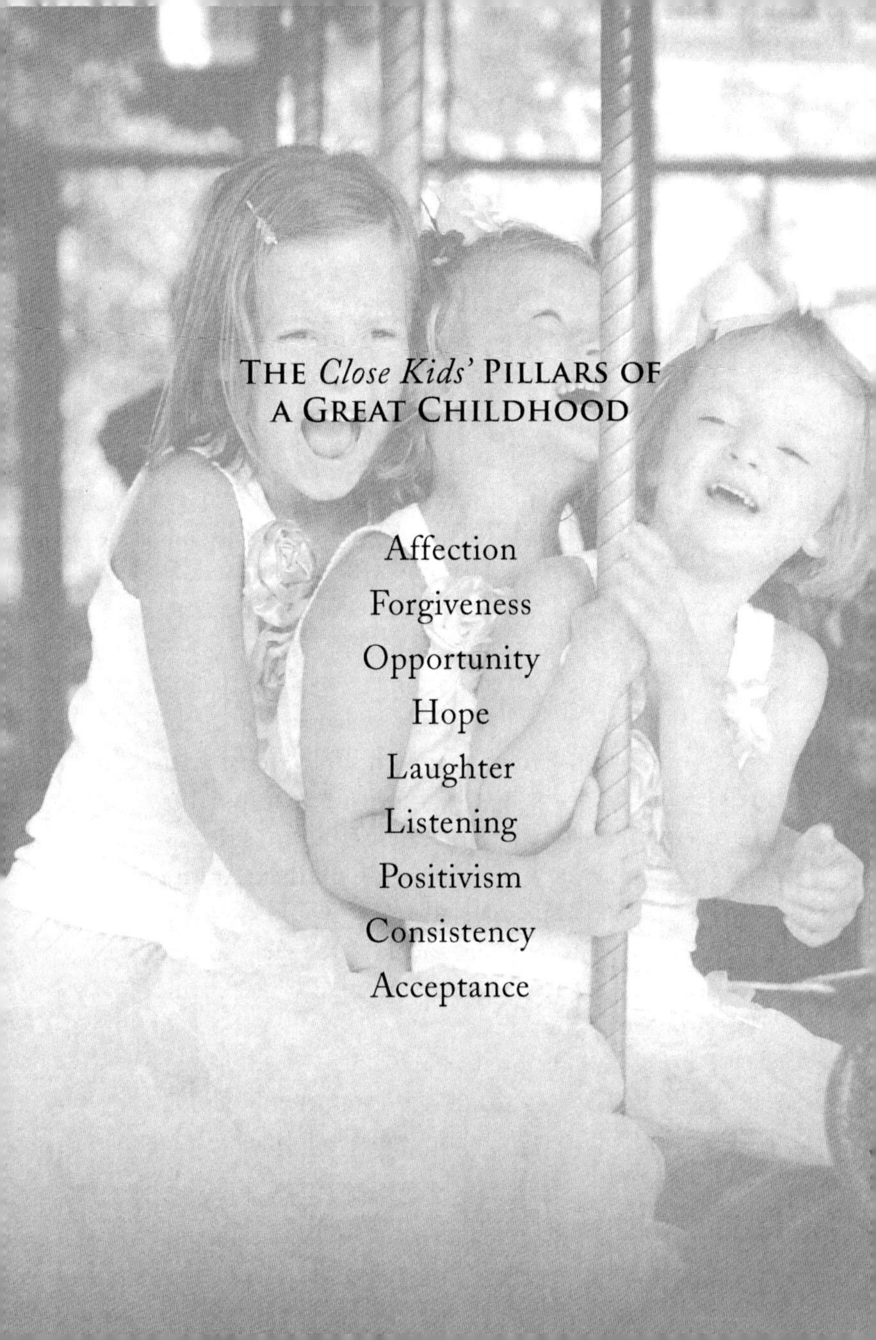

THE *Close Kids'* PILLARS OF A GREAT CHILDHOOD

Affection
Forgiveness
Opportunity
Hope
Laughter
Listening
Positivism
Consistency
Acceptance

AFFECTION

> Love has nothing to do with what you are expecting to get—only with what you are expecting to give—which is everything.
>
> —Katharine Hepburn

What is real affection? Is it touching? Telling our kids we love them? There are literally millions of ways to show affection. Some are based in genuine love, and others are not. Kids seem to have a way of sniffing out true affection.

As adults, we often encounter conditional affection, which is absolutely *not* what this section is about. It is so annoying when someone we know uses affection for the purpose of manipulation. They pretend to care and then end up asking for a favor or revealing an ulterior motive. Another example of conditional affection would be giving my daughter a big hug and kiss for cleaning her room. As parents, we want to heap honest affection on our children.

Some conditional affection will always be used by parents to teach children specific lessons. Teaching right from wrong and helping children learn about acceptable and unacceptable behavior is hard to do without a conditional "response" of some sort. But there must be a large percentage of time spent giving unconditional affection. A loving touch—hugging, holding, kissing, snuggling, etc.—should be a part of every child's daily existence. I don't think we ever outgrow this basic need either. I personally love affection received from my family and friends. We all do; it's in our DNA.

Healthy doses of loving words and behaviors can go a long way in making a child feel like a treasured part of the family. Parents should give affection because they want to, not to garner *anything* (even reciprocating love) in return. It should be a pure gift. So I challenge you to take each of your children into your hands and look them straight in the eye. Try saying the following: "I want to tell you I love you, and I think you are great!" Do it today. You will love the results, and so will they! True affection at its finest.

If you have trouble showing affection in this way, here is a simple idea that might help you. Try a family hug. Get everyone involved to make it a bit easier. Not ready for that yet? Start by holding a hand. I did not grow up in a touchy-feely house at all. But I married into a slobbery, kissy one. Let me tell you, the slobbery, kissy one is better! It took me a while to get used to it, but I'm there now and so are the kids. They totally followed our lead. They hold hands most places they go.

Have boys? Try lots of high-fives and encourage them to do the same. Some of my fondest memories (growing up with one brother) were of playing Wrestle Mania. The two of us and my dad would roll around on the ground almost every Sunday. Lots of wrestling, lots of tickling, and lots of affection.

Affection can also be shown with a simple squeeze, reading a book with a child on your lap, a nice walk in the neighborhood, or an "I Love You" note in a school lunchbox. Start small, keep it up, and encourage your children to do the same!

> Even though there are eleven years between my sister and I, we were, and still are, really close. She would crawl up on my lap while we watched TV or grab my hand when we left the house. I remember she used to come in to my room every time there was a thunderstorm. Many times I would wake up with her and ten

of her stuffed animals in bed with me. Her little head would be poking up from under the covers with a circle of little critters strategically placed around her head. These memories still bring a smile to my face all these years later.

—Craig
Phoenix, AZ

FORGIVENESS

> Forgiveness is the answer to the child's dream of a miracle by which what is broken is made whole again, what is soiled is made clean again.
>
> —Dag Hammarskjold

Think of the last thing your child did to upset you. Feel free to take a second. Try to come up with the one specific thing. Okay. Got it? Now ask yourself, "Have I done worse?" I'll bet your answer is not only yes, but "Yes, and much worse!"

I've personally seen parents get infuriated with their kids over accidentally spilling a drink at a restaurant. It appeared to ruin the whole meal, as the mood lingered on and on. Heck, I spill something every now and then myself. Why do we get so upset when one of our kids does the same thing? Their motor skills are still developing, and believe me, they do not concentrate on multiple areas at the same time very well.

Why do parents become so upset when kids do kid things? In our family, we have to constantly remind ourselves to lighten up (especially me). As the girls grow up, the problems we encounter will be more complicated and difficult to address. But I'm quite certain there isn't much trouble they could find themselves in that I have not been in myself. Forgiving and *forgetting* are good for kids and good for us. It frees us to move on. We can help our children learn this early on by requiring them to "kiss and make up" before they walk away from a conflict with their sibling.

I read on forgiving.org that during a conference on forgiveness in Atlanta, they claimed people who forgave others lived physically healthier lives than those who did not. They have lower blood pressure, lower cholesterol, and a host of other positive benefits. Children especially need to know that no one is holding a grudge against them for the mistakes they are bound to make. Freeing them completely from their errors (not to be confused with freedom from consequences) reduces artificial boundaries between all family members, resulting in better relationships all around.

Kids are going to make mistakes with their relationship just like parents do. What ties forgiveness to building a positive relationship between siblings is the same thing forgiveness does for a couple's relationship. It is knowing in your heart that past digressions will be kept in the past, not brought up to be used as weapons in future conflicts. If we practice forgiveness in our families, our kids will practice forgiveness with each other.

I received the following e-mail from a man named Daniel from Los Angeles. It said:

> Hello, Brett. I just received and participated in your sibling survey this morning. The timing of it marks the second consecutive day I've been reminded of my only brother. I'm almost seventy now and recently lost my brother a few years ago. We were great friends most of our lives but had a falling-out about ten years ago. He passed away before we could make amends, and it will haunt me forever. To my shame, I didn't even attend his funeral.
>
> Yesterday, I received the attached story in my community newsletter. After some thought, I'm sending it your way so it might help someone you come in contact with. From my own experience, I have learned it is better to both forgive and admit wrongdoing than lose a brother. I hope your project turns out great.
>
> —Daniel

Two brothers who lived on adjoining farms fell into conflict. It was the first serious rift in forty years of farming side by side, sharing machinery, and trading labor and goods as needed without a conflict. Then the long collaboration fell apart. It began with a small misunderstanding, and it grew into a major difference, and finally it exploded into an exchange of bitter words followed by weeks of silence.

One morning, there was a knock on John's door. He opened it to find a man with a carpenter's toolbox. "I'm looking for a few days' work," he said. "Perhaps you would have a few small jobs here and there I could help with? Could I help you?"

"Yes," said the older brother. "I do have a job for you."

"Look across the creek at that farm. That's my neighbor; in fact, it's my younger brother. Last week, there was a meadow between us, and he took his bulldozer to the river levee, and now there is a creek between us. Well, he may have done this to spite me, but I'll do him one better.

"See that pile of lumber by the barn? I want you to build me a fence—an 8-foot fence—so I won't need to see his place or his face anymore."

The carpenter said, "I think I understand the situation. Show me the nails and the post hole digger, and I'll be able to do a job that pleases you."

The older brother had to go to town, so he helped the carpenter get the materials ready, and then he was off for the day. The carpenter worked hard all that day measuring, sawing, nailing. About sunset, when the farmer returned, the carpenter had just finished his job.

The farmer's eyes opened wide. His jaw dropped. There was no fence there at all. It was a bridge, a bridge stretching from one side of the creek to the other! A fine piece of work—handrails and all—and the neighbor, his younger brother, was coming toward them, his hand outstretched.

"You are quite a fellow to build this bridge after all I've said and done."

The two brothers stood at each end of the bridge, and then they met in the middle, taking each other's hand.

They turned to see the carpenter hoist his toolbox onto his shoulder.

"No. Wait! Stay a few days. I've a lot of other projects for you," said the older brother.

"I'd love to stay on," the carpenter said, but I have many more bridges to build."

—Unknown

OPPORTUNITY

> Never tell people how to do things. Tell them what to do, and they will surprise you with their ingenuity.
>
> —George S. Patton

Opportunity falls in nicely after forgiveness. Children should be given every opportunity to show they can achieve greatness relative to their age and abilities. Foster Cline and Jim Fay (authors of *Parenting With Love and Logic,* Pinon Press, 2005) say that if a child has a 10 percent chance of completing a task, we should let them attempt it. Allowing them to try something new will either give them more confidence or allow them to learn from their failure. When I first started trying this, it was tough. Standing back and letting my child get frustrated trying something new was certainly not a normal parenting skill for me.

I hated to see my children struggle, so my tendency was to step in and help. But I became determined to let them try new things. A second thought hit me as well. If I do not let my children try to accomplish more on their own, it is the same as saying, "You cannot do this, so I'm going to finish it for you."The sound of that is actually quite horrible. How will she learn anything new if her own parents rob her of the chance to try new things? And frankly, parents should be the ones who are the most patient and most willing to let kids try, learn, try again, and succeed.

Now it is routine at our house to give the kids a chance to try almost anything. Even if there is really no way they can do it, they get to give it a whirl. I'll never forget one sunny afternoon last summer. It was about ninety-eight degrees, and I was mowing the lawn when a little visitor came outside.

"Daddy, can I mow the yard?" asked my four-year-old.

"Sure, honey. Come on over."

She couldn't even reach the handlebar, but she wanted to try. Hey, maybe she would surprise me and be able to mow the yard all summer! It didn't take long to realize it was not going to happen this summer for either of us—wishful thinking on my part!

She felt good about her opportunity to try, and she learned about her temporary limitation. Keeping their safety in mind, my wife and I let our girls undertake new things all the time. We've also seen how each subsequent child can do more things at a younger age than their older siblings.

There is no reason I can see to put artificial limitations on what is possible for a child. Frankly, no one knows what children can really do. No one! And I'm reminded often that my way is sometimes neither the best way, the right way, nor the fastest way.

Be prepared though! Two things will happen when you start giving kids opportunities to try new things. First, they will turn into little explorers. You taught them to innovate! They will, and they will surprise you with their tinkering. Sit back and watch the show. Second, they will allow each other the chance to do more and more different things.

After we started this, something very interesting happened. Our oldest two were heading off to color. We keep the art supplies in a box on the shelf just above a cabinet. The shelf is just high enough where the oldest was the only one tall enough to reach the crayon box. But this time was different. The oldest said to her little sister, "Why don't you try and get them?"

Try and try, but number two just couldn't reach the box. As number one was just about to step in, my little one got creative. She opened up the lower cabinet, stood up on the internal shelf, and reached the box of crayons. The look on my eldest's face was priceless as little sister came through.

HOPE

> He who has health has hope; and he who has hope has everything.
>
> —Thomas Carlyle

Hope is really just a state of mind for parents. Parents should always have hope that today is a new day—today is the day our children use their past mistakes and successes to make quality decisions to impact their lives in a positive way. This kind of hope ties in closely with forgiveness and opportunity and is the next pillar of a great childhood.

Hope makes today better by allowing us to believe that the choices we and our kids make *will* continually improve over time. It also says, "You know what? My children *are* still learning. They will make good choices today, and if not, they will learn valuable lessons from any poor decisions." It is these decisions they make, both good and bad, that allow kids to ultimately learn the difference between the two. They will also acquire confidence in their own ability to make choices—something that will come in handy as they become budding adults and peer pressure mounts.

Our hope and confidence instills hope in our children—we set the example. Where does your hope come from? Within? Mentors? Religious conviction? Giving our children resources/reasons to be hopeful should just be part of our everyday conversations and interaction with them. Hope specifically gives kids freedom. It puts the circumstance behind them and lets fresh ideas and new friendships flourish.

If there is a lack of hope on our part, other areas of our parenting—and life for that matter—break down. Hopeless people and parents make irrational decisions and desperate choices. No matter what situation you are in, hang on to the hope that the future will be better, for your sake and your children's.

Hope brings a positive attitude to children's relationships as well. To clearly see what hope can do, it is useful to look at the opposite, which is hopelessness. Hopelessness not only generates an overall poor attitude but leads an individual to isolation. Isolation of family members is the most hated enemy of any family whose goal is to create close children. It is better to try and avoid this up front by staying optimistic. Besides, we are all better off living life from this mind-set anyway. Try it on for size.

Laughter

> Humor keeps you in the present. It is very difficult to laugh and be disassociated with the people around you. In that one moment together you have unity and a new chance.
>
> —Alexis Driscoll

I can say with 100 percent certainty that I've laughed harder since becoming a dad than I ever did before having the little rug rats around. You know, the things kids do are really funny. For example, our twelve-month-old wanted to throw herself down and start a tantrum. Just as she was about to hit the bathroom tile, she decided to find a softer spot. She actually looked around, crawled over to a cushy mat, and threw the fit. That was hilarious for a twelve-month-old to plan out her own little escapade! At least we got a kick out of it, even if she did not. Her mother and I laughed so hard we cried, and the next thing we knew, she was laughing too.

My advice on laughter in the context of this book is simply this: laugh *hard* with your kids every day—real, kindhearted laughter. A prerequisite for this is learning to laugh at ourselves often. If you pull up WebMD.com and search laughter, you will find over one hundred articles on how laughter makes you healthier; opens up your arteries; and, according to a study by RX Humor, aids the immune system of children.

Playing tickle games is practically a daily ritual around the house. The kids love it, and so do we. Our day just seems better with a bit of laughing. And being able to look in my girls' eyes when they are laughing is a wonderful memory for me as a parent. I'm stocking up.

Laughter generates a spark in the memory that lasts forever. I remember back to many events where our whole family had some huge laughs together. They never leave me. The more time we can get our kids laughing together, the more opportunities we give them to create long-lasting memories and common experiences that further weave them together.

LISTENING

> If (children) feel listened to, they are more likely to be able to listen and will feel more understood, have more trust, and be more interested in what you have to say.
>
> —Gail Saltz, MD

Everyone knows being heard is vital to *any* individual's self-esteem. Imagine for a moment if you spoke and no one heard a single word you said. You would go crazy! You go to the grocery store, no one listens; to the doctor, no one listens; you call the phone company—well, that is *actually* what happens when you call them, but you get the point.

Think of it from a child's perspective, and multiply your frustration by about ten. When their voice is consistently ignored or only halfheartedly listened to, your child's self-esteem and sense of worth is diminished just like an adult's. They feel unimportant and even invisible at times. I constantly tell myself to stop and look at my children when they are speaking to me. It is not always easy. Believe me. They talk a bunch.

Marc Pittman, author of *Raising Cole* (HCI, 2004)—which I highly recommend, especially for dads and sons—talks about a special way he found to get his sons to talk to him. He calls them "Dead Man's Talks." The concept is really pretty simple. Let me give you an example. Let's say my daughter does something she knows is wrong. Instead of hiding it, she can come to me and say, "Daddy, I need to have a 'Dead Man's Talk.'" What this means is that I agree to listen to everything she has to say *and* respond to her as if I were a dead man. I'm not allowed to comment, make suggestions or facial expressions (this is really hard), punish her, or repeat anything she says to me.

Pretty cool concept, I think. I would rather have a child that is willing to talk to me when she messes up or just needs someone to listen to her than just about anything else. I love this idea! Although this is just a tool to open dialogue, teaching children to listen is critical for the relationship they are building with each other. Listening well to each other helps them avoid disagreements, stops fights before they start, and creates mutual agreement on sticky issues.

By the way, it can go both ways. When we, as

parents, mess up, it is important to let our kids know that we know we made a mistake. We might even ask for a Dead Man's Talk in return! By listening to our children and letting them listen to us, a bond of trust is built. A totally new level of understanding is reached that nothing else can match. Letting our kids be heard and teaching them to be good listeners to us and each other is definitely a pillar of a *great* childhood experience!

POSITIVISM

> Positive thinking will let you do everything better than negative thinking will.
>
> —Zig Ziglar

Although it should be obvious that being a positive parent is better for our children than being negative, putting it into practice is sometimes difficult. As *we* struggle at home getting three kids to everything on time, our outlook is not always positive either in word or deed! But we really try to control what we say within earshot of our kids.

My girls have proven over and over that they hear almost everything we say. They might not react to it, but they hear it. (You know what I mean.) If you don't think they are listening sometime, use this test. Say something they would normally "ignore" in a voice loud enough for them to hear. After they pay no attention, ask them in the *same voice* if they want a cookie, or say, "Ice cream is on the table." It is just like magic! See what happens? Ah, the results will *not* shock you. So they are listening, even when they do not act like it.

I'm also in the camp that believes children

construct their self-picture based on what *they* believe we think about them. In other words, our kids will only believe what we tell them if they know we really mean it. If I tell one of my girls that she is a great writer, then she hears me tell someone else she is a poor writer, which message will she believe? She would become confused by my two differing remarks and most likely think what I told *her* was not true. She might even call me a liar, and she would be right. Her trust in me would probably suffer as well—a brutal double whammy.

Strive to talk with and about your kids in the most positive light possible. There are usually several ways to approach any given situation. For example, let's look at a child who is loud in public. The pessimistic parent might say to a friend (usually in front of the child), "Lizzy is very loud, and I just can't take her anywhere!" This statement is not positive in any regard nor is it particularly constructive, and it only serves to reinforce the bad behavior. What is the point of saying these extreme statements about our kids anyway? Are we trying to embarrass them into changing their ways or cover our own embarrassment? I've certainly done this to my kids, but I'm trying hard to avoid it.

Here is an example of how the positive parent reacts to the same situation. "Lizzy is learning to use her indoor voice better every day. I'll be able to take her anywhere soon." It is nearly the same words but said in a much more positive and loving way. You might not see the difference during your conversation with your friend. But the message your child receives will be both positive (the compliment) and constructive (the fact she is learning to be better).

Why badmouth your child anyway? Would you say something like that about a friend standing next to you? "Mike here sure is a loudmouth, and he often smells bad, but he is great to have in a golf foursome." Listening to it, it sounds silly, don't you think? Shouldn't we treat our own kids with as much respect (if not more) than anyone else?

Use this method to discover whether or not you are a generally positive parent: Just listen to yourself talk to your friends about your children. Do you consistently bring up the bad things they do instead of all the great things they do? Do you share good stories about your children with others? Are you your child's best advocate?

Our society seems to have shifted from parents overbragging on their kids to parents overcriticizing them. As a child, I remember people saying things like, "Mike and Ilene are always bragging on their kids. I hate it when they do that." Well, we may have gotten what we wanted. Being critical of parents who "brag" on their children has caused the pendulum to swing back the other way.

"Little Mike doesn't listen."

"Angela throws her food."

"Cindy is so loud at restaurants."

Come on. Who wants to live that way? We all have to remember that kids are just that: kids. Our expectations as parents today are sometimes out of proportion to their true capabilities in many different circumstances. Let's keep it light, fun, and positive. It *is* going to keep getting better every day!

This specific notion is very important in your children's life and relationships together. It is subtle but very powerful. If parents talk consistently negatively about a child for any number of reasons, the other siblings begin to process what they are hearing. It is very similar to advertising a message over and over again.

Let me use the previous example of "Cindy is so loud at restaurants." This statement is most likely said within earshot of all the other siblings. Everyone knows being loud at a restaurant is bad, right? So if Cindy is loud and loud equals bad, it follows that Cindy by definition is bad and irritating. To the rest of the siblings, the message heard was, "My sister is bad and irritating." So the next time there is conflict between Cindy and a brother, the brother might start with the notion that Cindy is already bad and irritating. Using this as a starting point during conflict makes it very hard for Cindy to ever reach a successful resolution.

Think of a pendulum that is simply hanging at a neutral six o'clock. Because of her parents' negativity toward her, Cindy might start the next clash with her brother with the pendulum starting on the negative side instead of at the neutral position. Instead of looking for understanding and a quick resolution about the specific problem, Cindy must first prove she is not bad and irritating (thus just making it back to neutral). Only now can she fairly start to work on the actual issue at hand.

This makes it really tough to find common ground solutions.

This message is not to beat parents up for a slip-up. We all have our moments. This is intended to reverse the pattern of anyone who *consistently* treats their children with a high degree of negativity. We have to all focus on what is going right today. The residual value you will see in your kids' lives is well worth your effort.

CONSISTENCY

> Our children are counting on us to provide two things: consistency and structure. Children need parents who say what they mean, mean what they say, and do what they say they are going to do.
>
> —Barbara Coloroso

There are really two kinds of consistency to think about as a parent. First, being the same person from day to day and situation to situation. This is extremely difficult. I often find myself acting or reacting differently in very similar situations. For example, one of the girls should be asleep, and instead she is up and playing. How do I react? I know I'm not consistent with them, and I really struggle with this kind of situation. They should have some general idea of how I will react, don't you think?

As human beings, we experience good days and difficult days—sometimes things just do not go our way. The ebb and flow of life can spill over and make parents act rather poorly when we normally would have given the proper response in a given circumstance. My fear is that inconsistency on my part will lead them to pull away from me. Not knowing which Daddy will show up could make them avoid me altogether.

The second form of consistency is purposeful deception. I'm afraid this goes on more than we would think. These are the parents who act one way in public then make a 180-degree turnaround behind the walls of home. If you find this describes you or your spouse, consider talking to a professional about it. Children who live in this environment (with the double standard of "Do what I say, not what I do") need to be able to trust you to be there for them, protect them, and get the problem fixed.

Consistency relates directly not only to our children's association to each other, but parents can see it in their adult relationships as well. Consistent people, or those who are reasonably predictable, are easier to be friends with, and inconsistent, unreliable people are simply not easy to be around. I would bet you have very few unpredictable friends in your life that you spend much time with. It is just too hard.

If we are consistent with our children and teach them to be consistent as well, it makes them more equipped to be a good friend, a good business associate, and more importantly, a good sibling.

ACCEPTANCE

> Do not train a child to learn by force or harshness; but direct them to it by what amuses their minds, so that you may be better able to discover with accuracy the peculiar bent of the genius of each.
>
> —Plato

Acceptance was intentionally left for last because it is so important to the well-being of the family. My plea can be summed up in this sentence:

> Let yourself and your family be fascinated by all the differences in your children, not frustrated by them.

There was no greater commonality in those survey respondents who did not have a good relationship with their siblings than the following: *they felt no one in their family cared enough to try to understand them.* In their minds, they were too different from their parents and/or siblings to be liked, appreciated, or loved for who they were. The price they paid for their differences, real or perceived, was alienation both mentally and physically *for life.* They were ultimately separated from the ones who should be most forgiving and accepting of them: their own family.

It is so difficult to lead our kids when they truly need it and let them find their way when they are ready for freedom. But ultimately, it is their life and their choice, so at appropriate times, we must let go and try to enjoy the ride. I'll never forget a line from *My Big Fat Greek Wedding.* It touched me, and I have never forgotten it. As the daughter in the story struggled with falling in love with someone "different," her mother helped her with a liberating thought.

She said, "I gave you life so you could live it."

In essence, she told her daughter, "I accept you whatever choice you make. And on top of that, you should accept yourself as well." Wow! I will never forget the strong impression that statement made and continues to make on me.

Each of our children will make thousands of decisions long after they are out of our care. Those decisions will affect their life, their family's lives, and the relationship they ultimately have with their siblings. My hope is the more they learn from all of their experiences today, the better prepared they are for tomorrow. As a parent though, it is hard to sit and watch them struggle sometimes as the learning process unfolds.

Regardless of their choices, my wife and I have committed ourselves to accept them as kids and later as adults no matter what—even if we do not always approve of what they are doing. We even tell them that very thing regularly. When the prodigal son came home after squandering his wealth, his family name, and his personal reputation, his father did a courageous thing. He accepted the son's admission of wrongdoing and welcomed him home. Anything less would be anything less.

> Hello, a friend sent me your sibling survey and I have a response to your question, "What would you have done differently to have a better relationship with your siblings." It can be summed up quickly, but I think it is totally true.
>
> I would be more tolerant of our differences.
>
> Plain and simple, I let minor differences, not even bad ones ruin my relationship with my brother. I can't even explain why I was intoler-

ant, but I was and it ended all hope I have to communicate better with him. I'm trying desperately to teach my granddaughters to love the things that make them different and not make the mistakes I made.

—Matt
St. Augustine, FL

A LAST GUIDING RULE

As I looked over these nine traits, I came up with one guiding rule of parenting that helps me make tough decisions and creates a productive environment for kids to forge their relationship. This rule applies regardless of how difficult the situation my children are involved in is or how much I want to bail them out of a mess. After reading it, see if it helps you deal with some of the difficult choices you have to make.

> Parents' Golden Rule:
>
> Parents are responsible—in *all things,* at *all times,* and in *every situation*—to do what is in the *best interest* of their children.
>
> Super Important: We parents never outgrow this responsibility!

Sound reasonable? The hardest part of the equation is the two words *best interest.* When is it best to let my child suffer through a mistake for the purpose of learning a lesson? Is the cost of the lesson in line with the amount of anguish they are experiencing? To me, this is one of the biggest dilemmas of parenthood. I, like most parents, want to keep my girls from all pain. But the lessons (pain) they experience from a mistake would probably qualify as being in their best interest. Also, the cost of a blunder to a young child pales in comparison to the cost of a mistake as a teenager or young adult. As tough as it may seem, let them learn early!

ABOUT QUALITY TIME

You may have noticed that I have not said anything about *quality time.* It was intentional. If you look at the pillars of a great childhood we discussed, they cannot be given to a child without spending a great deal of time with them. So if you concentrate on the pillars, you get the quality time *free!*

In today's fast-paced environment, we spend a large amount of time running from place to place with our kids. Parents try to do everything, and we forget to do the most important thing of all. That is doing *nothing* with them. I think the official CloseKids definition of quality time is doing absolutely nothing *with* your kids. There is a great slogan of a popular hammock retailer, and I love it. It says, "Accomplish nothing." Classic!

Please shoot me if you ever hear me say, "I spent some quality time with my kids today working on their algebra homework." While this is probably a very good use of time, what was the focus? The homework. Being with the kids is certainly better than not being, but we can do better.

Here is the kicker and the absolute silver lining. It is really what makes this idea so fun to implement. What we think are insignificant or meaningless activities, our kids see as golden time. To say this another way, when I watch Barbie and Ken get married for the hundredth time this week (shouldn't once be enough?), desperately trying to stay awake during all the kissing that is coming, *that* is the time my girls cherish the most.

Alvin Rosenfield, MD, a child psychologist and co-author of *The Over-Scheduled Child: Avoiding The Hyper-Parenting Trap* (St. Martin's Griffin, 2001), says that family time is being sacrificed today for a whole host of other things. He cites a study showing unstructured activities have dropped 50 percent over the last twenty years. Family dinners have dropped 33 percent, and family vacations are down 28 percent.

We all have to work hard to accomplish nothing with our family. I believe times like this are invaluable to parents who want to connect to their children, children who want to connect to their parents, and ultimately the children connecting to each other. Time with family where nothing else distracts you may be the most enjoyable activity you ever do together!

Playa Los Ayalas

There was a fisherman who lived in a small, coastal city in Mexico called Playa Los Ayalas. His name was Jose Javier Garcia. Jose was known far and wide as the most successful angler in town. He went out every morning and caught his daily supply of yellowtail to be eaten by his family or sold at a "temporary" market. He then traded for other items the family needed. And every day, rain or shine, he always came back with fish—always.

Jose was a very happy man. He enjoyed leisurely afternoons playing with his grandchildren, tinkering with his boat, or taking a siesta as the sea breeze blew by him and his small home near the beach. Jose routinely turned down lucrative offers from successful businessmen to guide them on fishing expeditions. They begged, but he always said, "No, thank you."

One bright, cloudless Monday morning, after returning from the sea, Jose was met by a young, well-dressed gentleman. He was in his early thirties, with a small portfolio in his hands. In it lay his plans to make our storied fisherman rich. It held a detailed strategy how, with Jose's legendary fishing reputation and some hard work, they could build a fleet of fishing boats. They were destined to become the largest and most successful commercial fishing company on the Central Pacific coast.

When the young businessman finished his presentation, Jose had a question.

"Why would I want to do that?" he said.

"Well, you could be the richest man in town and have everything you have always wanted."

"But why would I want to do that?" he repeated.

The businessman replied, "So you can retire, enjoy time with your grandkids, play with your boat, and laze around your house."

He kindly said, "No, thank you," as he walked away and smiled broadly. His heart was warm because everything he always wanted he already had. Jose lived a very simple but very rich life. Many of us are probably a lot like Jose; we just don't realize it yet.

A Final Real Change

The heart of the Matter

There is one last thing I learned on my journey that could not go unsaid. After pouring over my information for years really, something hit me. Almost all sibling problems are rooted in one thing. That one thing is selfishness.

Greed, jealousy, needing attention, and inability to understand others all have roots in being selfish. "I want it my way and no one else matters."

I wondered what could be done in my children's lives to affect their tendency to act this way. Then I came across the story of six-year-old Zach Bonner, and the solution hit me right between the eyes. Let me tell you about Zach for a minute. He is an ordinary kid from Florida. He heard on the radio that people in New Orleans needed water after Hurricane Katrina hit. He set out with a red wagon into his neighborhood to collect water to send to Louisiana. He ended up sending twenty-seven truckloads of water.

Zach has since walked 280 miles to raise money for food in his hometown and done countless other things for his community and the people who live in it. His actions are the epitome of unselfish behavior.

I believe we can change the hearts of our children and reverse our natural, self-centered nature by actively giving our time to others. In fact, this has become a real passion in my home. My kids might never become another Zach, but they don't have to either. Doing small things for others is what I'm really after.

There is so much anecdotal evidence of children who take the time to volunteer having a very high degree of love for each other and everyone around them. There are abundant acts of charity our children can participate in *with* us. *With* is emphasized because parents must model the new behavior by working alongside their children. It also provides us with fun, heartwarming tasks to accomplish as a family.

There are so many positive benefits to charity work! Not only are you helping an individual, family, or group in need, but the benefits to you and your family are immeasurable. Throughout our lives, we have heard, "Giving benefits the giver more than the recipient." They were not just talking about money. In fact, I think giving time is just plain better. Your time is probably the best contribution you can make to another human being.

It is this kind of generosity, shared by parents and their children, that leads to a generation of youngsters with strong, caring souls. I mean, what kind of kid would be a bully one day at school and go help pick up trash at a shelter the next? The two just do not go together.

After all, in the end, who really cares how good of a soccer player, piano player, or dancer our children become? I'm pretty sure none of that ultimately matters. Most activities our children are involved in today will not even be sustained much past adolescence anyway. But spending time helping others can result in a lifetime of soul-feeding activities for your family!

Here are some initial ideas of charitable tasks parents and their children can do together.

- Buy and distribute gifts or food during the holidays to needy families.
- Take a few new stuffed animals or balloons to a local children's hospital. If you really want to go crazy, help your kids save money to hire a clown for a few hours in a children's unit. The kids will forget they are even in the hospital! Call the pediatric department for more ideas. Tell them, "My children and I want to do something for the kids in the hospital. Do you have any ideas?" Whatever you decide to do though, *check with the recipient before you actually show up.*
- Take some used but not used-up toys to a pediatric oncologist's office (or any pediatrician's office) for their waiting room.
- Draw pictures and mail them to a children's hospital or to overseas military personnel.
- Deliver a meal or a snack to someone in your neighborhood totally out of the blue.

Try this. Get some tiny pretzels, put them on a cookie sheet, and drop a Rolo™ on top. Put them in the oven at 225 degrees for about five minutes. Let your kids press down a pecan half on top of the soft Rolo™. Put them in the refrigerator for a few minutes; then deliver them. These are super easy, taste great, and are a fun way to get into the giving spirit.

- Color a picture or card for the retired, single person down the street.
- Check with your church for activities they have already started. There are always charitable events taking place there.
- And there is so much more! I'm trying to start an idea database on the CloseKids.com blog. Check there to add your own or see the latest!

My personal goal is for each family that reads this book to choose only one action item to accomplish each quarter with your children. That is a few hours once every three months! Again, consider how much time we spend developing our kids' bodies by taking them to soccer, gymnastics, basketball ... on and on. Then we help develop their minds with school, music lessons, and reading. Again, on and on. This is all perfectly okay! But let's not entirely skip over arguably the most important element of the human experience: *their souls.*

Traditionally, we, as parents, don't take the time to help develop this priceless part of a child, and it shows in the world around us.

I hear it already. Some people will say, "We take our kids to church every Sunday. Isn't that enough?"

No, it is not enough. It is a great start, as religious services lay the groundwork to learn right and wrong. But the next step is to apply those principles we learn inside the church walls to our lives outside of them. Practically all religions have elements of giving in them. Is there an excuse for any of us to learn and believe in things we are not willing to practice?

Ultimately, the benefit of giving things away is beyond measure! When kids learn to give to the less fortunate on a consistent basis, something in their heart clicks. They care less about the small possessions they used to fight over. Children become more likely to share with their brothers and sisters. As adults, they are more likely to give to the community and be involved in helping those around them. This is truly a lifetime gift to your children and everyone they come in contact with. Please, just give it a try.

When Hillary Clinton became first lady, she gave a speech about a new discovery she made. She learned there were bigger things in life than her. That is the exact thing we want to teach our kids! There are bigger things in life than ourselves, the kind of car we drive, the house we live in, or the clothes we wear. The real key is to start teaching this to kids at age six—maybe even sooner.

Also, I really did not even mention how these acts of goodwill help the recipients of it. There are people in every city, town, and community that need real help *today.* It is not the government's job or someone else's job to improve their lives or give them hope; it is our job. Sometimes, a simple thought from another person can totally change the outcome of a person's day, week, or month. Good deeds have a way of lingering on. So, please, start planning ways to reach out to somebody in your community today.

The bond created by the family who donates their time is unbreakable. In my opinion, husband and wife with brother and sister helping in their community unites their hearts and souls to each other.

Our family started working with an organization called Santa's Cause every year during the holidays. The girls look forward to collecting toys, wrapping them, and ultimately delivering the toys to kids. They talk about it for days afterwards and remember every December to ask about it. Our hope is this shared experience will teach them the joy of service, the realization of how fortunate they are, and the fact that they can do great things while being together. Now we are in the process of finding more we can do for others.

Is your family looking to help someone in your community? If you don't know where to start, these Web sites can point you in the right direction.

Compassionatekids.com
Kidscare.org
Habitat.org/youthprograms/
Hud.gov/kids/kidsvlta/
Takepride.gov

Epilogue: A Final Story of Hope

I've been waiting for the right moment to interject my personal story. After completing the survey and compiling all the data, various sorts were performed to find trends or answer some specific questions. In one of my sorts, all respondents were ranked from those with the closest sibling relationships at the top of the list all the way down to those with the most distant at the very bottom of the list.

I was at first stunned then a little saddened to see the name on the very bottom of the list, literally the last name on the bottom of the page, was my own mother's. How sobering it was not only seeing someone I happened to know in that position, much less my own mom.

When I began to think about it though, her childhood situation was anything but stable. She grew up mostly on her own. She would go to movies by herself in Dallas, Texas, at the age of five! Her brother and she were not close in age and were truly as different as night and day. Neither one had a father figure in their lives to help them either.

After I had time to digest it a bit more, I became very proud of my mom! She proved that the chain could be broken. Where she rated her overall childhood experience a 2 of 10, I rated my own childhood a perfect 10. She performed a near complete turnaround in one generation! She made the effort and took a stand that my brother and I would not grow up in a broken or loveless home, and *she did it!*

We were not unique in how we grew up in middle America, so there was nothing particularly noteworthy to tell you about my childhood. We were not the poorest family in town and certainly not the richest. My parents sacrificed one thing for me: their time. I could not have asked for anything more.

I shared this story for one reason. So you will know the future of your family is in your capable hands. You have the power to continue building on your positive work or set a new path for your family and your children if you need to. They will then continue to practice what you have taught them for generations to come because they learned from the best: you!

Remember, anything in this life is truly possible, and we all have the power to change our lives for the better. So make it happen.

I want to end by saying thank you for your support of this book. It is truly humbling and an honor you read it. May you and your children realize all the potential and joy God intended for you.

APPENDIX

ABOUT THE 10'S

Here is some additional information that surfaced right as this book was going to publication. The numbers are interesting to me and worth passing on to all the analytical readers out there.

What if you looked only at those people who rated their adult sibling relationship a perfect 10? Are there any significant findings? Some of these tendencies are intriguing, and I will let you decide their importance.

Here are the findings of the "Perfect 10s:"

- They have 2.7 siblings (or there are 3.7 total kids in the house)

- They have only 2.7 years difference between the oldest and youngest
- They talk to their siblings 2.1 times a month
- 90 percent said their mother was close to her siblings
- 78 percent for their fathers (Dads, we need to fix this.)
- 88 percent thought their parents were fair
- 65 percent thought they were strict
- They are currently between thirty and forty-five years old
- 18 percent went through a separation or divorce
- 81 percent had a stay-at-home parent until all siblings went to school
- 36 percent lived in a house where both parents had a college degree
- 80 percent would refer to at least one sibling as their "best friend"
- 93 percent would tell you they are close to all their siblings

- 50 percent said they fought "a bunch" as kids

Whew! That is a bunch of numbers! More information like this is in the works for the CloseKids.com Newsletter subscribers. It is free, so come join us when you get the chance!

FURTHER INFORMATION

Additional information about the author and other resources for readers are available at *www.closekids.com.*

Contact information regarding speaking engagements or media inquiries for Brett A Johnston is also available through *www.closekids.com.*

e|LIVE

listen|imagine|view|experience

AUDIO BOOK DOWNLOAD INCLUDED WITH THIS BOOK!

In your hands you hold a complete digital entertainment package. Besides purchasing the paper version of this book, this book includes a free download of the audio version of this book. Simply use the code listed below when visiting our website. Once downloaded to your computer, you can listen to the book through your computer's speakers, burn it to an audio CD or save the file to your portable music device (such as Apple's popular iPod) and listen on the go!

How to get your free audio book digital download:

1. Visit www.tatepublishing.com and click on the e|LIVE logo on the home page.
2. Enter the following coupon code: 982e-a1bb-e49a-1e28-5506-c06d-4a94-d060
3. Download the audio book from your e|LIVE digital locker and begin enjoying your new digital entertainment package today!